Read for a Better World™

MY SCHOOL COMMUNITY

A First Look

KATIE PETERS

GRL Consultant, Diane Craig, Certified Literacy Specialist

Lerner Publications ◆ Minneapolis

Educator Toolbox

Reading books is a great way for kids to express what they're interested in. Before reading this title, ask the reader these questions:

What do you think this book is about? Look at the cover for clues.

What do you already know about a school community?

What do you want to learn about a school community?

Let's Read Together

Encourage the reader to use the pictures to understand the text.

Point out when the reader successfully sounds out a word.

Praise the reader for recognizing sight words such as *my* and *the*.

TABLE OF CONTENTS

My School Community . . . 4

My School Community

My school is a community.
We learn and play together.

A citizen is a person in a community. It is important to be a good citizen.

What rules does your school have?

I follow the rules.

8

I raise my hand in class.

I listen when someone else is talking.

I try my best to learn.

I help my teacher.

How have you helped
your teacher?

I put things away
when I'm done.

I help kids in my class.

How have you helped
kids in your class?

I share with kids
in my class.

I make new friends.

What do you do
with your friends?

19

I am a good citizen at school!

You Connect!

What is something you like about your school community?

What do you do to be a good citizen in your school community?

What other communities are you a part of?

Social and Emotional Snapshot

Student voice is crucial to building reader confidence. Ask the reader:

What is your favorite part of this book?

What is something you learned from this book?

Did this book remind you of anything about your school community?

Photo Glossary

class

friends

school

teacher

Learn More

Bassier, Emma. *Manners at School*. Minneapolis: Pop!, 2020.

Gates, Margo. *Making Friends at School*. Minneapolis: Lerner Publications, 2023.

Heos, Bridget. *Teachers in My Community*. Minneapolis: Lerner Publications, 2019.

Index

Photo Acknowledgments

The images in this book are used with the permission of: © ESB Professional/Shutterstock Images, pp. 4–5; © Prostock-studio/Shutterstock Images, pp. 6–7; © Monkey Business Images/Shutterstock Images, pp. 8, 10, 23; © Twinsterphoto/Shutterstock Images, pp. 9, 11, 23; © wavebreakmedia/Shutterstock Images, pp. 12–13, 18–19, 23; © Oksana Kuzmina/Shutterstock Images, pp. 14–15; © Igisheva Maria/Shutterstock Images, p. 15; © Liderina/Shutterstock Images, p. 16; © antoniodiaz/Shutterstock Images, p. 17; © Ground Picture/Shutterstock Images, p. 20.

Cover Photograph: © Shutterstock Images

Design Elements: © Mighty Media, Inc.

Lerner Publications Company
An imprint of Lerner Publishing Group, Inc.
241 First Avenue North
Minneapolis, MN 55401 USA

For reading levels and more information, look up this title at www.lernerbooks.com.

Main body text set in Mikado a Medium.
Typeface provided by Hannes von Doehren.

Library of Congress Cataloging-in-Publication Data

Names: Peters, Katie, author. Title: My school community : a first look / Katie Peters. Description: Minneapolis : Lerner Publications, 2024. | Series: Read about citizenship (read for a better world) | Includes bibliographical references and index. | Audience: Ages 5–8 | Audience: Grades K–1 | Summary: "What does it mean to be a good citizen at school? With full-color photographs and leveled text, young readers will learn what it looks like to be a part of a school community"–Provided by publisher.
Identifiers: LCCN 2023002364 (print) | LCCN 2023002365 (ebook) | ISBN 9798765608715 (library binding) | ISBN 9798765624616 (paperback)| ISBN 9798765616543 (epub)
Subjects: LCSH: School environment–Juvenile literature. | Citizenship–Juvenile literature.
Classification: LCC LC210 .P48 2024 (print) | LCC LC210 (ebook) | DDC 371.5–dc23/eng/20230223

LC record available at https://lccn.loc.gov/2023002364
LC ebook record available at https://lccn.loc.gov/2023002365

Manufactured in the United States of America
1 – CG – 12/15/23